THE
THE IMMORTAL SOUL
SALVAGE YARD

poems by

Beth May

SIDESHOW
MEDIA GROUP

8033 Sunset Blvd. #164   Los Angeles, CA. 90046
sideshowmediagroup.com

SSMG PRESS / LOS ANGELES

The Immortal Soul Salvage Yard
Beth May

Cover Art by Lauren McKay

SSMG PRESS copyright ©2021

Sideshow Media Group
8033 Sunset Blvd. #164
Los Angeles, CA. 90046
USA

sideshowmediagroup.com

THE IMMORTAL SOUL SALVAGE YARD

CONTENTS

My Resume (For the Benefit of Future Lovers)   9

Love Letter to the Body in Tempe Town Lake,
or The Immortal Soul Salvage Yard   12

Does the Family of Florida Man   15

1. Static   16

2. Electric   17

You Were Just a Wave   21

Flat Earth   22

Love Part Two: Prologue   25

Love Part Two: Epilogue   26

So Much Better   28

Story Man   31

Be Kind For Everyone You Meet is Fighting a Hard Battle   32

The Actor's Nightmare   34

Love Part One: Future   35

Write One Like Dean Koontz She Says   38

Emails to a Professor in 2011   40

This Might Be Fiction   45

Dark Times & Deeper Sympathies   46

The World is Ending and I Have to Tell the World   47

There Never Was a Hat   49

The First Time I Watched Pornography   53

My Book Report! "If You Give A Mouse A Cookie"   54

3. Rhyming Dictionary   55

4. So She Explains   57

Stay   58

Overshare   59

An Explanation   61

Woman!   62

Help Wanted Sign in the Ladies Restroom
in a Cafe in Flagstaff, Arizona   67

Long Distance Call   68

Psych Ward Sunflower   71

Chiropractor   74

May   76

My Father Writes About Hunting Dogs and
I Hear His Voice for the First Time   80

Afterword: Notifications   82

Thank Yous   85

About the Author   87

All of these poems are inspired by physical pieces of the past. Some are reincarnations of older poems or stories, and some build a bridge from old mistakes to current cringe. All of them (in a way) are recycled. All of them (in a way) are new.

You know the saying. One person's trash... is that same person's book of poetry.

Beth May

MY RESUME
(FOR THE BENEFIT OF FUTURE LOVERS)

EMPLOYMENT HISTORY

At my old job my shift manager asked me about my five year plan. I do not have a five minute plan. I have five minute smoke breaks that I have wasted by not taking up smoking. My dad once walked in on me smoking a cigarette and made me smoke a whole pack and now every time I have sex I fuck a guy like my dad will walk in and make me fuck 25 more.

SKILLS

I am a humorist. I am a downer. Sometimes at night my thoughts are like skittish dogs that cross my path. And I know that if I try to call them back they will not come. I like to write thank you notes and lie. I'm both tired and adventurous. I am loud and so scared. I am cold to the touch and if you hold me too long (please don't, please don't)— I get lonely at night but I wouldn't have it any other way and when you hire me I won't mean to make you jealous I just like to brag about places I may have never been, things I may never do. Let me do them with you.

EDUCATION

I applied to Harvard with a letter of recommendation
I wrote myself. I wrote a suicide letter on my 23rd
birthday. I wrote a letter to explain to the boy that
I no longer loved that I had run out of metaphors
for the texture of his hair. I wrote a letter that said,
*please do not consider yourself broken. You are just a
mirror with a crack that I see every time I look at my
reflection.* Please do not consider me gone. Please do
not consider me gone. Please.

REFERENCES

Reese McNally says that I am "a shining example of
a hard worker." Mom said that I was the smartest
person in the whole world. Mom said she never lied.
Mrs. Seitz, my 3rd grade teacher said that I showed
proficiency in math (Mom said she was just being
polite (but Mom sometimes lies (I hope that doesn't
damage Mom's credibility as a reference))). Don't
trust anything that bitch Cheryl says. Reese McNally
says that I am "an excellent addition to any team."
Cheryl thinks I'm making up the positive testimony
of Reese McNally. I think Cheryl should shut the fuck
up.

PHONE NUMBER

Please note I've attached a phone number at the bottom of the page so you may reach me for an interview. I hope you can reach me. I have no area code. I am just defending this area below my collar bone. I am building up my contacts like making any human connection is a contact sport. Please contact me. Please follow up. Please check to make sure my ribs rise and fall with my breaths, sinking into old fault lines like enemies that fall back into this familiar bedroom every time. Please hire me so I can claim experience and wealth. Please fire me so I can claim experience and wisdom. Please look at this resume so I can know I'm alive. I'm alive. I'm alive. I was the last one to know but the first one to apply. I'm alive. Please consider me.

Beth May

LOVE LETTER

TO THE BODY IN TEMPE TOWN LAKE, or
THE IMMORTAL SOUL SALVAGE YARD

One morning I got up

I got up early because Arizona State University had
a rowing club that
sucked so much
they put me on the team even though
I sucked so much
There was a small police boat
in Tempe Town Lake and
it's more like a moat and
we didn't know it then but
they were looking for you

Sorry

I mean your body
they were looking for somebody's body
It had released you from its grip
You slipped into waters way deeper than this
man-made lake and there
spirits are lining up to find god
and do you think we'll ever find him?

The team and I joked
about a Phoenix mafia that doesn't exist
disappearing into the night after
disappearing you
I called you a risky suicide
The bridge isn't high up
The water is warm in August and
the team hated me so bad when I wasn't joking

I read
where you probably just got drunk drowned
in that warm water

I said I related

My coxswain said what and

I said I related

I knew what it was like to pass
off your soul to strangers
like a bad Goodwill bucket hat
I knew what it was like to want it back
but to be stuck between decisions with a head
so naked
I said I related, like a lot
I am related to you

And I read they did two autopsies on you so

I said I related

Nobody said what

I said I related

Because I too have been passed
between people whose lips were like hotels
with short term hospitality
I too have come to conclusions
that it wasn't foul play

I didn't want to tell you this
but we had a full morning of practice
that day
and nobody asked your name
I never tried to find out
I didn't want to haunt your ghost
to write a bitchin' obituary
snuck into
a form letter template short and way too polite

It's so weird
how we start off as strangers to everybody and that
it can almost be like that again

I am an acquaintance to everybody

DOES THE FAMILY OF FLORIDA MAN

Come forth to claim his body from the mouth of the alligator he was trying to fuck

And if so is there a closed-casket funeral

And if so do his coworkers leave the funny bits out of their eulogies

And if so do they laugh in secret with crumbs on their lips from crackers from the wake of a man nobody knew from birth as they know in death

And if so do they drive drunk with grief, and does the grief hold them upright by their throats as they talk to the cops with flashlights on their pupils

And if so does his widow bail them out

And if so how far away can she get

Does she reveal his death to neighbors on airplanes

And if so does she tell the whole truth

And if so do the ears of coach class perk up

And does that neighbor keep the secret

And does his widow realize his secret doesn't belong to him anymore

| STATIC

Ok, so a girl walks into a bar and tells you that she's a flashlight or a candle, and she thinks about that for a second and says no she's more like an old outlet on some family's dry-docked speed boat that they barely use and then the girl asks for water and beer and says the reason she says this is because she was once something Electric, and actually the girl is just me and there's nobody in the bar, there's no bar, but I was once something Electric. I say I think about this a lot on the I-10 Westbound late at night until I hit the 405 South and put the brightest parts of the city to my left I say I think most about Electricity when I've got nobody to shock but myself I've got nobody to blame but myself I know nostalgia's a hell in itself but it's cheap enough for frequent vacations.

I am almost 28 and my skin is hazy tan with light pollution after an Electric 9 years. I can't figure out why I want to glow again. I can't justify returning and romanticizing the worst moments of my life like a Lifetime Channel film or a TED Talk or a Poem. I write these poems with a tourist visa to hell and I promise not to stay. I promise not to stay. I promise I'm ok, but I used to be Electric . So...

2 ELECTRIC

Stop me if you've heard this one before
I got a twin size mattress just big enough
for me and the lord
but sometimes we fit one more, and I only got fitted
sheets and pillow cases
Don't need more sheets more excuses
to shake this fabric loose
wrap this neck in a cute microfiber noose

Don't worry

I lose thoughts like that
when I'm under the quilt with someone new

Stop me if you've heard this one before
I said I got a twin size mattress, never used
I got ideas got plans for things I'll never do
I got so much fucking energy no insight no view
Stop me

I used to pray
I used to be caffeine free
I used to be a good student with straight a's,
a rolling backpack
Sometimes I forget too much to remember
what I want back
Recently I forget too much
I forget too much

Stop me if you've heard this one before
I used to be Electricity

I knocked on strangers doors
like a good-time-ending policeman
the first time I felt it
Electric
bottle of Fireball in my fist, lazy thirst
gulped, never sipped,
then it was half gone and I was full gone
the voice of fucking god fucking egging me on
I had no choice
Don't you see I had no choice
but to turn into Electricity?

I used to be crazy
I used to stay out all night
because I worried that twin sized mattress
might look too appealing
Like I'd waste the high sleeping
Like I'd have a good time dreaming
Like my sanity wasn't worth keeping
I used to fall in love
my love, like a hairbrush through bedhead
the way it pulled out strays
touching each piece so painfully, individually
I used to fall in love
I used to swallow men
down

I used to burn bridges faster
than I could build them
up

I used to try and explain
explain this Electric tendency
to rip tags off hairdryers
and dip my future in water

I used to try and explain
I used to say oh I'm just a southpaw blacksheep, this
family's personal arsonist
and you will never understand
I will always have to explain
I used to be so insane

I used to be in denial
  (no I wasn't)

but whether it set me aflame or it set me aflame
I used to treat an illness like a game

I used to let the cycle of down ups cradle me like a
shaky pair of glass arms
I used to be so shocked at the drop
I used to get my brain shocked and I don't know how
to explain
the way my brain sometimes feels
like it is on fire
the way I am when I am
my family's personal arsonist

I will never be able to explain
that even when my head feels
damp and cool underwater
I want to go back into the fire
again I'll always want to be Electric again
So stop me if you've heard this one before

Stop me if you've heard this one too many times

I got a twin size bed just big enough
for me and the lord but sometimes
we fit one more and so often
there's room for many more and so often
I'm only wishing you and me could fit again
I'm not that static anymore

I hold other people now
and it's too short less Electric now
the fuse is longer now

I remember the last 9 years
no better than I remember my own creation
I think about salvation now
I think about salvation

YOU WERE JUST A WAVE

the ghost that haunts Grandma
howls and rattles chains
but she is too far gone

to notice that she is the ghost
and we are too far gone

to admit we had the keys
to the chains we are

far too close
with Grandma's ghost to feel it
haunting us anymore but it
won't ever stop

FLAT EARTH

A woman outside
of a coffee shop in Santa Monica said I reminded her
of her mother.
That surprised me, because I didn't give her a good
look at my face I was facing away thinking
she'd ask me for change.

She said that I had her mother's blue eyes and her
chin.
She said she knew that, like her mother, I was also
working with a government agency to harvest her
neurons for leaders.

I sat down with her.
Didn't get her name
or the name of the alien planet she'd reclaimed from
the sun.
I didn't tell her that I played a game just like this
one,

Except the sun rises out of
the Grand Canyon in my
game and can you see it?

And **NOBODY** fucking knows
this because nobody can see it
like me
          because it's
                a matter of depth perception

It's a matter of light deflected
It's a matter of life and death
It's a matter of time before
this happens again

I sat down with her.

She said, yeah
her mother had blue eyes like mine.
She said a good government clone is hard to find.
I found myself talking to a landmine
sunk so deep below ground that her explosion
wouldn't shake the surface at all.
If the Grand Canyon holds the sun in,
then there are worse places to fall.

When you're crazy, the whole world is so far away
that it doesn't matter if the earth
is round or flat.

The poet talks insanity,

as if it's romantic like that.

LOVE PART TWO: PROLOGUE

In poetry love is a metaphor
In life it's something you wake up for

The sun in poetry warms and lightens us
The sun in life burns our retinas

The sun wakes the earth, disappears, repeats
We sleep under blankets when we lose the heat

I've been covered in SPF 10,000
because sunburns don't forgive
But I forgot without sunlight almost nothing can live

LOVE PART TWO: EPILOGUE

ABC traffic report is of a family of four
crushed to smithereens
in some
four wheel drive sporty suburban with big doors

One of those
just-5-minutes-to-grandma's-house
wrecks that nobody expects
But I expect because this is a metaphor but I'm
nobody's grandma
Nobody's
but I still feel the weight of that big car
sitting in my lap
sometimes

I feel like a wreck
the aftermath of a collision
And nobody has been
colliding with me for a long time
but he used to say he was fine like
he knew I knew he was not fine
used to say nevermind like
he knew I'd ask again I always asked again
I wonder if he's finally fine now
that I'm not asking

Because I'm nobody's grandma and I live more than
5 minutes away
and you can take your time
Got so much time to be fine now
That fine head of yours could be mine now

but I'm sporting some
four wheel drive sporty suburban with big doors
Just a metaphor, but I'm saying it's
a time machine these days

I'm not asking you to stay, he said those days

I spent eight months curled up
next to a survivor Of a wreck
I came to know well and
I'm nobody's grandma but
I put my thumb on his neck, pinched some artery to
stop the blood
But it never stopped, kept me warm,
filled my lungs And we were a wreck
No clue where we were bleeding from
The blood felt so heavy

That's fine I said, a lie
I'm fine he said, a lie
My fingers slipped, a lie
I'm nobody's grandma but I'll die
My fingers grip my own veins again,
a lie, sometimes
My fingers are cramped
like hard noodles or straws
The noodles don't fill him
The straw does not empty him of worries

His blood didn't keep me warm so long

Beth May

SO MUCH BETTER

You could have it so much worse
they told her with blood
rushing down her thighs at an emergency room in
Cleveland, Ohio
didn't know the name of the man who did this
three drinks and a kiss
too fast
she said no

No

NO

but he kept going
beat her ears like eggs and flour till she forgot
the way home
moaned compliments as he finished
like it was a team effort to get him
off

the doctor wrote a prescription for Plan B,
said it was lucky she wasn't hurt seriously
great thing you aren't single raising some bastard's
blue-eyed baby

Some people have it so much worse

You could have it so much worse
they told him as he scattered
his wife's ashes off the coast of Blue Hill, Maine
where a westward sea wind
caught them
pitched them back
into the sand like a football spike
she went nowhere even in the afterlife

and he thought a little that she deserved that
leaving nothing
for him and his two sons but a sorry
note and self-slit throat
but the gatherers at the wake said
he was lucky
hell man she coulda been murdered
mowed down by a motorcycle

this was her
choice

move on

Some people have so much worse

Beth May

You could have it so much worse
they told her while she was scooping up
a plate of peas at Walter Reed
diagnosed with PTSD because she
lived when others did not
Afghanistan is not only hot
during the daytime

she tells them how the pop of artillery
embraces her brain like her own thoughts
what 10 pints of human blood looks like
soaked into the desert's crust
they respond with how lucky she is with
all her organs all her limbs

could be sleeping in an American flag
coffin but congrats soldier, you made it home
Some people have it so much worse

We could have it so much worse I'm telling you and

If

this hurts & I'm drowning I'm a weak ass feather
in the wind ~~ please call my water dangerous
make me strong enough to swim

Story Man

Out of necessity he became a parody
Dog fur man laying with wolves
In the bed where his wife once slept
The bed where his child
Escaped nightmares and dozed
Between bodies that turned the bed
Into a fortress keeping out the world

And when he wanted the other world
He leaked out of theirs and out
Of necessity the
Wife wondered if she caused the spill and
Out of necessity the child wondered if he
Would ever stop leaking

Out of necessity they turned him into a character
Into a story man
A joke butt
Into a poem
Where his villainy took shapes
Felt solid, merely beyond the reach
Of their empty hands

And together they turned him
Into art
Because although he was out of love
He was still in the picture
Out of necessity they continued to paint him

Be Kind FOR EVERYONE YOU MEET IS FIGHTING A HARD BATTLE

Be kind, for everyone you meet is fighting a hard battle

Be kind unless they are not

Be kind unless you are aware of the battle and you don't think it's a very big deal of a battle

Be kind unless their battle is at war with your own battle

Be kind unless others are watching

Be kind unless the ones watching are wanting a battle

Be kind unless you are butter-side down, other side of town, bad guy now

Be kind if the good guys are kind

Be kind unless the good guys cannot abide your kindness to bad guys

Be kind unless you doubt their name, their photo, their past, their privileges

Be kind until you doubt them

Until the kindness hemorrhages and you hate them

Be a kind of resentment that smiles back

Be the gentle attack

Meet back at the kindness again

Be kind of angry

Kind of horny

My kind of man

Your kind of a Saturday night

The kind that takes time to kick in from the pill

And myth goes mankind never flew so high

Myth goes broken heart's a bad kinda way to die

Be kind

Be kind

Be kind

Be kind for everyone you meet

Is everyone you meet

Is everyone you meet

Is everyone you meet

Beth May

THE ACTOR'S Nightmare

I fall asleep telling a lie
I fall asleep wanting attention
Wanting to part a curtain of hair from some stranger's ear and stir trouble
and once I have that I wait for applause
They hold their applause
They all know I'm only here for applause I fall asleep wishing to be utterly invisible and
they applaud my enemies
with hands shot toward hands
like hooves like earth like heartbeats
And I fall asleep so scared I dream
I know this is a dream I will fall into again, a loop
on a screen, a grizzly screen and a murder I will not stop
I fall asleep witnessing everything and saying nothing I shut my mouth with
a creak like a mailbox and I am so lost in the dream,
no address here
Pay no mind give me no attention
make my memory an enemy

LOVE PART ONE: FUTURE

Years before we meet
I will write you this break-up poem
Maybe I think it's more romantic that way?
Really it's more dramatic that way, and you'll soon
find that I'm the girl who can look in a mirror longer
than a two term presidency
The girl that looks at you only to know where to look
The girl asking how the movie ended when she
dozes off
Look, look
I will doze off on top of a—

And this might be fiction but I think
I'll see you coming
I was the girl who said "thank you"
like the receiving end
of a tornado warning the first time I got cat-called,
but I am wary now,
That girl grew teeth from gift horse mouths
I'll see you coming
but I'm not sure how
I'll hold out until you—

Of course,
before this poem there will be others.
I'll compare your body to the bible, write that I need
that good news
Look, look
I'll make such a view of you

won't stop to see the real thing up close but it will
be such a view
There will be precious few
moments I'm not writing a fucking poem so look
while we still—

Then, soon, you'll know me
How I fall into lust so easily
Likening my short attention span to the long days of
spring
When really I just get chilly feet
And I'll write you a—

The life won't be steady
The certainties will be small disasters,
re-introductions, shrugging shoulders
Bad thanksgiving casseroles
I will be the girl who announces she is straight edge
after snorting powder from straight razors
I will be fine, only in the spaces when you are not
fine,
Which is not as lucky as it sounds
These disasters will sound like a—

It will be so good to save us when we are good
When I am not the girl getting speeding tickets on
bicycles
And when we are the people who don't remember
that girl
When we call each other "mine"
Look, look
We will be fine before—

The girl will call you from someplace she's never
been
She'll win
I'll write you this break-up poem knowing how love
Gets scarred by all the skin we touch
Look it takes so much
It takes so much to—

Spend another year thinking about the spiders we all
swallow in our sleep
Is it 6 or 7
And I will let you down
Take you into my mouth
Wrap myself in my own web while we both
Stomp on spiders that do us no harm unless—

When it's over
Look, look it's all over
No harm done but the girl doesn't give as much love
to the mirror, to her shadows
I will write you into a sandwich, describe only your
crusts
And this might be fiction but I'll still feed you plenty
down the line
I write this poem for when I'll love you
But when you're not mine
Look, I still—

Write one like Dean Koontz,
SHE SAYS

Write one like Dean Koontz
write one that is much
much farther away
write one that will require my reading glasses
something to fill my time
on a plane
or at a hairdresser
or inside a house
write something that is not here in this house

can you write something
that I can slip away after
can you write me a hole to sink into without
ever writing about the hole I sank into
and remember
when I sank I didn't warn you
didn't mention
that you would sink in too
write me a reason to read
a way to forget
write me out of the theme and back in the
dedication

write me
if you must
so that I am utterly unrecognizable

with slicing reptilian eyes and three cheeks no
dimples
and a beginning to return to
or write me out

she says I love you sweetie
but write one like Dean Koontz

or write me out.

EMAILS TO A PROFESSOR IN 2011

WINTER

Hello Professor,
My name is Beth May and I am in your Tues/Thurs
lecture class. Unfortunately I will not be able to make
it to class today, as I am sick with a bad cough that
would disrupt class. While I'm aware that your syllabus
mandates that all absences are considered
"inexcusable" without a doctor's note, I was unable to
get a doctor's appointment until next Monday. Given
the circumstances, I hope you understand and might
make an exception to excuse this absence. I'm really
enjoying your class and (knock on wood) this will be
my one and only absence.
Thanks,
Beth

Dear Professor,
So sorry for the late notice but I'm still feeling under
the weather. I will bring a doctor's note when I return.
Thank you,
Beth

Hi Professor,
I am unfortunately unable to come into class today. I
have a flat tire - likely a nail from that darn
construction on Apache! I will get the notes from my
desk neighbor Ben.
Apologies,
Beth

Hi, sorry. My desk neighbor is actually Shawn.
-Beth

Hey Professor,
I will be absent from class today as I need to attend to
a family emergency.
Thank you for understanding.
-Beth

Professor,
I know what you're thinking, "So many
grandparents die when projects are due!" lol but the
thing is I really do have a death in the family. It's my
great-grandma, so not even
part of your joke lol. But it is serious and I am
grieving!
Thanks for understanding!
-B

Hi,
Gonna be
Absent today.
Regular grandma died.
:(
-B

Hey,
I think
I'm onto something
really important, like a scientific discovery of my own.
Will be absent until I reach the
conclusion.

Can't get out of bed professor it's early and cold and I want the covers on top of my ears like an upside-down hat, like the beanies with the little ties, you know?
Those ones.
Can't.
Can't get out of bed.

Prof! I know you dropped me from the course but I'll be in today with my results.

Hello I can't find them.

Hello I can't find the classroom.

Hi the door in my dorm is a whole room away, over carpet and you know how carpet gets crumbs when you eat pop tarts? My feet feel like that professor. My feet. I'm standing on crumbs of pop tarts and nobody is toasting me nobody is putting me in the microwave the microwave the microwave just 5 seconds and I'll be ready 5 seconds and I'll explode I blow a hole through my headboard and onto the pavement below I think I have been leaking jelly since birth, leaking the jelly of a too-toasted pop tart placenta and I was tied tied around my mother like a backpack strap, too long and loose, or maybe a fanny pack womb
and I thought you were my mother professor but you were just the wave.
You were just a wave.
Waving to you!
Beth

Professor I can not get out of bed when are finals.

Professor I can not get out of bed what time does class start.

Professor I can't move can I write a lab paper on paralysis.

Can I use retina technology to write words or form little rhombuses that you can understand to prove it's me professor it's me.
I'm so sorry and I've tried not to be but it's me.

Can ya shoot me prof? Don't got a gun here.

Nvm prof I got it covered.

Professor I will be absent for the rest of the semester, as I will be dead.
Hope you understand.

Professor I am freezing and all I want is that upside-down beanie hat with the little ties.
The ear flap things.

SPRING

Greetings Professor,
My name is Beth May. I'm not sure if you remember me, but I was a student in your Tues/Thurs lecture class last semester. I unfortunately had to drop your class mid-semester and take some time off of school for a family emergency, but I'm back and eager to get back to learning! I loved your lectures and I'm confident I'll get a lot more out of them this semester. I will be late to the first lecture unfortunately as my car is in the shop and I am unable to arrange commute alternatives, but otherwise I am sure my attendance will be perfect. I hope you understand.
Thank you!
-Beth

THIS MIGHT BE FICTION

I'm nobody's baby I'm
I'm just a born again navy brat
best belonging to different zip codes
I've never been home long enough to call it that
I think I was born with invisible tusks on my
forehead
To carve my own welcome mats into my neighbors
porches
I am everybody's neighbor and
Nobody's wife
Nobody's stick of super glue
Nobody's lunar guiding light
In fact I'm not that sticky at all and
Sure you can catch me and hold me upright but I'll
probably fall eventually I'm sure we're gonna fall
eventually
So I'm nobody's baby I'm just a liar coughing
nervous pebbles out my lungs
I betray myself break myself
Cutting out my tongue's the only time I kissed
something else
Break my nose my toes will step up and learn how to
smell
I can see you clearly though
Finally
I been blocking an awful lot of light
I'm so cool
I been blocking an awful lot of light

DARK TIMES & DEEPER SYMPATHIES

At the store you pay for the sad card knowing you will do all the real work yourself. Sure there's sending it, finding a stamp that isn't an American flag in the year 2020. The full extent of the work doesn't hit you until you pick up the pen and realize that this card, covered in cursive sorrows and flowers, is too formal for anyone really until they die. Until they die and the card in your hands cannot write their name for you.

The card leaves empty space at a time that is otherwise occupied, full, over and it's not a comfort. It's another space to fill. The body slopes into a grave and a hand grabs the collar of a t-shirt until it is full and there's nothing else you can grab. There is no room for you in grief. There is no job to complete but there is work to do.

You pay for the card you write the words that find them in this dark time and they read the words or maybe they just set the envelope aside and you wonder if the words can help and they wonder are there words that help and there once were words on someone else's lips that won't open ever again and there is nothing you can do until the day the letter finds you and the cursive turns the letters of your name back into alphabet slots as formal and as far away from you as the day you were born, before you got scared of the work you need to do.

THE WORLD IS ENDING

AND I HAVE TO TELL THE WORLD

The world is ending and I have been selected
to deliver the news.
It's not my pleasure to do so
but it's an important duty
and I want to do this right before I d-
Before all of us di -
Before we -

If you're reading this, now you know.
Mission accomplished.
I tell my mother via telephone, and though
there is no good way to deliver bad news
she seems to take it well. I hear
the whoosh of her head nodding,
the sound of her tongue against her teeth as
her throat holds onto a wail and I hang up quickly so
that she can release it. I know she will
tell my brother, who will google
whether the world is ending.
When google says the world is ending
he will text me,
tell me that the world is ending like it is his mission
to tell me and
not the other way around.

I ask if he has told his young son.

He says no.
I say good, good, keep it that way
and when the news spreads I add
a hashtag to my twitter posts.
I try to tell my former classmate but she
is convinced that the world will not end and I
am exhausted.

I'm glad the world will kill her.
I'm glad the world will kill me.

I receive several articles
with headlines peeking out from their tweets, gated
in by 280 words, not nice words,
but the good word in these is that
the world is not ending.

And though it is my job to know for sure
other people seem just as sure that I
do not know the things I know
and I wonder what their job is,
and I wonder why I wonder
whether the world is ending at all.

THERE NEVER WAS A HAT

I wanted to write you a love poem

In 2012
We go to a Christmas party together
You fish a hideous reindeer sweater out of your
mom's closet
Four sizes too small
Your collarbones peek out at me like little detectives
And we are suspicious of this but

In 2012
We fall in love

In 2013
I tell you I'm sick
I use a polite phrase
"Mentally ill"
You begin asking if I'm okay as if you're checking
the weather
You become so wary of hurricanes even when I'm
just a light breeze

In 2013
We sculpt our conversations into hilarious inside
jokes
We are so stupid cute together that someone ought
to punch us
We fuck like glaciers, like we have all the time in the
world

In 2013
I read all those love poems I used to think would
never apply to me

In 2013
I wanted to write you a love poem

But in 2014
The hurricane comes
You ask if I'm ok
But I am dying like a glacier
Melting in increments so slow
That you are the only one to notice
My hair and my face become thin
I'm so close to ripping the veins out of my skin
And then

In 2014
I get 38 consecutive treatments of electroconvulsive
therapy

In 2014
I wake up
You are driving me home from the hospital.
I admire the way your collarbones peek out from
your shirt like little detectives
I ask you what your name is
You look terrified

In 2014 I forget 2013

In 2014
"Mental illness" fades into the background with a
death rattle that sounds like every memory I have of
you
Our love becomes a set of keys stuffed in
yesterday's pants
And I try so hard but I cannot retrace my steps to
find it
I try so hard but I can't
Remember
Remember
how you tried to make me better
You offered to wear my scars in your skin, funnel
my shocks to your brain
I tell you this is my problem
I am ignorant of your pain
We start pretending that we dreamed this
We're two puddles who don't believe in rain

In 2015
We stop pretending
You go to New York City to find an apartment
But actually you find yourself
I get shipped out to Los Angeles
With a framed photograph of us looking happy
that I keep for three more years
I wanted to write you a love poem just the way you
remember it
But I don't remember it

In 2017
I write this poem anyway
I dream that one day it will find you
Remember your name
You see, your name is the worst kind of dream
That dream I don't remember when I wake up

THE FIRST TIME
I WATCHED *pornography*

12 years old with floppy socks

and insomnia

flipping through channels

at Grandma's house

on a television set

much older

than I was I came

across a movie

called SPIDERBABE

it had nothing to do with spiders

and I stared

at that first panoramic penis

like it was a car wreck

it whispered in my ear with explicatives that referred

to genitalia using words I once used to describe roosters

I was certain

I knew

at 12 years old

what love looked like

My Book Report!
"IF YOU GIVE A MOUSE A COOKIE"

If you give a mouse a cookie
he will ask you to marry him

He will say it is the logical next step
You will agree
Say no to the milk and yes to the dress

If you say "I do"
you will do it in Las Vegas with his mouse stepmom
and 2 coworkers watching

He will never say thank you for the cookie
You will never offer another
You will return to a house with no plan and no
leftovers

If you give a mouse a dish he will put it in the sink
and forget to wash it

If you give a mouse a reminder he will grow bitter

If you grow old with this mouse neither of you will
remember the taste
of a cookie
with milk
through a straw
for forever

3. RHYMING DICTIONARY

If she uses the big girl words to describe his hands, hands like the fit of expensive backpack straps, how their weight on her body makes parting from him an act of evisceration, why then does her professor's name escape her?

And how can she answer that question without googling some synonym without crying without explaining this thing that will take too long to explain?

She can't remember your name and you know her too well. She'll have to explain.

> I can't remember your name right now, she says.
> I have problems with my memory, she says.

But there's more to explain.

> She says, it's a side effect from a treatment.

And that's fine. She isn't obligated to explain she isn't obligated to do anything she cannot remember the word "obligated" or the word "tangible," or the actor from Die Hard that she mentioned 2 minutes ago and she isn't obligated to use the word "aphasia" but it's the only big girl word she remembers consistently and she wants to use big girl words again wants to be a writer again wants to be a friend a student a poet a member of the waking world again, so she explains.

> The treatment is electroconvulsive therapy, she says.

Also called ECT but it's a lot safer than it used to
be, she says.
It's not like that movie...that one with the...with
the hospital...and the man who...um, she says.
But it's helped me a lot, she says.
I cannot remember and it's called aphasia, but
this is the only thing stopping me from getting
electric again.

After 68 treatments of electroshock she is no longer
Electric and cannot place the word "irony" on her
tongue, like maybe there is more to explain.

Now she explains to wipe away other explanations,
the places minds can go to after hearing something
like that, the places of the minds of her friends that
might see her as the bottom of a lake or the floor of
a bathroom or the top of a building or in your mouth
on your body on your list of missed calls on your
list of people you have to explain yourself away
from with understandable lies.

I have work, you lie, a flat tire, you lie, grandma
died you lie

So she explains. Collects the little germs of life from
her own breath to offer you, an acquaintance.
Explains that she forgot your name because she's
forgetting a lot of things because her brain is being
electroshocked because her mind is electric because
at 19 she went crazy because it was the first time
she found god because it was the last time she felt
normal because she wants to be the kind of person
who remembers a name but she can't.

So she explains.

4. SO SHE EXPLAINS

When someone asks me what it's like to be crazy
I say that's a very rude thing to assume
next question please

When I want to tell someone
what it's like to be crazy
I do it unsolicited and starved for attention
and they always give me their attention when I say
that being crazy is like being a surge of Electricity,
when I say it got me every good poem I ever wrote
when it's got me talking about nudity and landmines
and dead mice and when it's got me
howling with my crossbite into an open mic

When it's got me hoping this thing
that's almost killed me so many times
just might be the thing that pays me to survive

I call up crazy with rowdy words to make it
sound more interesting than sane
(but the world's most boring place is inside my brain)
because I went crazy at 19 years old
and it was the obvious kind of crazy,
the I see gods in my dreams without sleeping
brand of madness that starts off
all those true crimes stories about cult leaders
but I think I'm most mad when I remember
no madness is the same
so I always explain

STAY

Stay

When I say that I blame her for staying,

I don't mean it like some kids mean it. I don't mean it in an angry way or the lost way where we blame our hometowns for having the nerve to call themselves home. Ya see, neither of us ever had an area code to call our own. And both of us look down into our palms sometimes like we're psychic fortune readers because you can't blame your hands for anything you can't predict.

She's old now and getting older and instead of waiting for her to get bolder sometimes I'm just waiting for her to get bold at all. There have been times in life where I felt like a fruit fly trapped inside a pantry, only waiting to see the light of day so that something else could kill me, so that the sky could watch me move on and she has always been there for me. Sometimes she doesn't understand the metaphors and most times there's nothing to understand but she can't stand to see me cry on stage or even page through a sad short story. She can't stand it. She can't stand it.

When I say I wish we could get by without it I'm not talking about anyone in particular.

OVERSHARE

I share that I am a Capricorn, and that I'm not sure what that means but whenever I read lists of famous or fictional Capricorns, I see some and say 'Yep, this sounds like me' and I see some and say 'No way.' He shares his sign and I forget it immediately.

He asks me to come over and I share that I have a hard time sleeping some nights, but he says he does too and we fall asleep with the sheets twisted around our knees like listless boa constrictors. I wake up at 3am, and he doesn't. I don't live here and I'm restless; the snakes around my kneecaps are constricting again but I don't want to move and wake him up because I am not ready to share that it's 3am and I'm awake. I leave early in the morning, frustrated, as if he's done something wrong. He thinks he's done something wrong.

I share that my old guy has a new gal with eyes the color of a recycling bin.
I share that I woke up at 3am. I let him know he has done nothing wrong.
I share that college was a little crazy and he says he went a little crazy in college too. We share a laugh about that.

I share my fries and he says

"Wow these fries are so good!"

but actually they're not.

I share a favorite movie of mine and he is restless. Snakes around his ankles are constricting him now and he wants to leave, but he doesn't share this. I wonder if I've done something wrong.

I share that while held for evaluation in an emergency room, a doctor closed a cut in my shoulder with medical super glue that didn't hold. I knew he should have stitched it instead

but I did this to myself. He shouldn't have wasted time patching up someone who clearly didn't give a shit about the scar.

I share that I give a shit about the scar. I share how my teeth nibble each other in panic every time I see it in the mirror.
He shares his big sweatshirt,
long-sleeves,
cavernous hood.

AN EXPLANATION

the **DAYS WITHOUT INCIDENT** clock
resets to zero after almost a year
I find pants to wear
something...
summer-y?
as summer-y as pants can be?
and I try not to think about it but here you are
you are white,
new,
pink bits,
and angry edges
and as much as I avoided your arrival
I am so excited to take care of you
to wrap you up
clean you off
sneak quick peaks at you as you grow
ugly and settle
I'll watch you improve and I'll be hypnotized,
proud, even, better!
look how much better!
much better
you improve, you improve and it's
because of me
and I will of course hide
you from the world but only because
what looks worse to the world looks better to me

WOMAN!

I went to a friend's bat mitzvah wearing a
Playtex pad soaked with the first blood that
didn't get cut or scraped out of me, but it still
hurt.

I can't remember her name, she's not a friend
anymore, but she became a woman then. And I
happened to become a woman on the very
same day. How strange.

There wasn't a pamphlet,
a tutorial,
a test prep text or a coffee table book.

I don't think there ever will be.

I don't have a daughter.

I don't want a daughter.

Because if I do I'll have to teach her things that
got taught to me.

Someday she'll teach her daughter all that I
taught her and she'll never teach her enough.
There will never be enough to teach her.

Teach her how to be a woman.

Teach her
  that you should send your smile
  to straight someone's eyeballs,
  black pupils swallowing up your
  teeth like bits of meat on a
  plate. Your teeth should only
  bite the bits of meat on your
  plate. Teach her the mouths of
  women can't bite anything else.
  Teach her that a smile is
  infectious but teach your
  daughter that Her smile is an
  antidote and the world will
choke on
closed lips
if she does not give it up.

Teach her that a smiles signifies respect
before she knows what respect is
and who it belongs to and who she belongs to
and where she belongs.

Teach her these answers before she asks
questions,
and she'll never know what we never knew.

I was lucky to have this all taught to me, but I
never learned anything I didn't see. So that
can't be my daughter, and it never could be.

I want to teach my daughter something new.

Tell her the stuff I wasn't taught.

Never teach, just tell her...

I'll tell her, a woman should consider her duties and
her place
Sink into your role which is woman which is you
which is weaker sex,
subservient,
second place.

I'll tell her, take those thoughts
and shove them up the nearest dick hole.

I'll tell her masculinity can be fragile, because the
privileged always fear the power they've lost to
equality.

I'll tell her,
      stop believing the lies you are told in
      inspirational self-righteous facebook
      statuses of friend of friends.

I'll tell her to breathe.

I'll tell her, find the one you love.
I'll tell her, lose the one you love.
I'll tell her love loses you sometimes,

and maybe you are left hanging helplessly like the laces of shoes tied over powerlines.

I'll tell her there will be other shoes to swing over your primary wires and it's okay if nobody is ever tall enough to fill them.

I'll tell her I'm sorry

I'll sit her down and say, look, I'm sorry for all the time I spent thinking I was not strong enough.

But I'm so sorry about the darkness, how it followed me home some nights like creepy car headlights in a horror film.

I'm sorry I've worn my own skin like a disposable halloween costume. It is just so fucking itchy.

I'll tell her to live.

> Live in your own skin.
> Stare at your veins from the outside in.
> Please live.
> Please find yourself.
> Play hide and go seek with yourself.

Please remember yourself when you wander.

We are all growing up in someone's else hometown.

I don't want a daughter, but just in case,

I'll hold her face in my hands and tell her this.
I'll tell her so many things. I'll teach her nothing.

I'll tell her to look in the mirror and learn what she sees.

I'll tell her the woman in the mirror is the perfect woman to be.

HELP WANTED SIGN
IN THE LADIES RESTROOM
IN A CAFE
IN FLAGSTAFF, ARIZONA

Please HELP! I want to kill myself

I sent in my resume never heard back
Backseat driver tucked in someone else's hearse
galloping over more graves Gardens grow salty
over the feuds in their roots
And you're stepping on my grave while I've got my
tongue on you

I hope a woman in a restroom can get some help
I hope I'm truthful in sayin I'm feelin well
I hope that we can stay here a spell
Just stay here
With our necks in belts

Tied over this stranger's fan in a hotel room outside
of Flagstaff
No chance for room service
No turning back
Change into the bathroom stall girl
so fast so fast so fast

Flush it down flush it down
Stay for now

LONG DISTANCE CALL

They say distance
makes the heart grow fonder but they never finished
the sentiment

I'm popping letters
into a mailbox
trying to figure out fonder of what?
You can't fondle shit inside absent thighs
while the delivery guy's
asking where Utica is

New York
It's in New York

I'm 2,393 miles away

standing on the sand to your snow
counting the days till you get home
begging you to fuck some sidewalk snowman and
give it my name
stick the carrot where it fits

The distance is making a 2 minute phone call fonder
but our voices sound different on the phone

The distance is making the fondness' freedom
harder and sometimes freedom
goes by John or Jerome and those guys
they give me winks without knowing

how hard this heart is owned by you

They can't take me home

They are not my home

I hope this letter gets to you

And on the phone your voice sounds different than
the night before you left

Your eyes were razors on my lips
I probably still had
bits of lasagna in my teeth but
I wanted to taste you too

I know it's late where you are

You've got no one to come home to
and I've got nowhere to go

We are separated by miles and mindsets like two
cross Atlantic countries that are too young to
declare war yet and you're looking at the sunset
while I ain't had mine yet

How's it looking tonight?
How are you looking tonight?

And on my twin-size mattress
when we pretended you weren't leaving
breathing in a synchronized sunrise
strangle-holding these final moments
of some harmonized timeline

I love how love is a word
that only its consumer defines

So I still love you when I'm two hours behind

When my sun rises with the heat and yours is cloudy
with sleet and you're forking down eggs while I'm
snoozing away
How's it looking today?

How are you looking today?
You've got no one to come home to and I've got
nowhere to go
I'm not going anywhere
Call me on the phone and just whisper
Whisper in my ear

I'm not going anywhere

PSYCH WARD SUNFLOWER

in the psych ward the rugs are made of fruit punch
stains and fingernail clippings
flipping out during group therapy sessions is cooler
than the radiohead lyrics that comprise them
television is less censored in catholic school

this is my fault my fault my fault my fault my fault
my fault my fault my fault my fault my fault my
fault my fault my fault my fault my fault my fault

my partner in my forty-eighth consecutive game of
scrabble asks me why
why die
my nurse asks to check my vitals and I say I'm fine
I'm fine I'm fine I'm fine I'm fine I'm fine
I'm fine I'm fine I'm fine I'm fine I'm fine
I'm fine I'm fine I'm fine I'm fine I'm fine
I'm still alive I'm what you want I'm still alive

so why and
it's weird

you don't get flowers in the psych ward

you get narrowed eyes, pursed lips asking
how you tried
and nobody ever calls suicide by its name and
they gave my roommate six diagnoses but suicide
is supposed to be vague

we ask to go back home and very rarely think
about why we came it's just hard to explain
we think only of card games and the next break from
routine, like a meal or a chance to look at the street
or a meal or a chance to look at the street or a meal
or a chance to look at the street
we look at the people on the street
and all I can think is those people can still be me
those people
you people
could end up just like me

me
I spit out twenty-seven pills of lithium
swallowed a little scream
I wrote vile, mean notes
and then I threw them away

acting like
that kind of hatred
don't stain the whole page

some days I am a stained page
some days I'm not this vague
I go to sleep some nights too heavy for my mattress
still submerged in a box spring
when I wake up some mornings
I still wake up some mornings
as if swallowing lithium is a battle cry
not a way to die
and why live
not a way to die and why live not a way to die and

why live not a way to die and why live not a way to
die and why live not a way to die and
why live

when at the sunniest part of the day
I can still see my shadow
I cannot shake it
I cannot shake myself awake
but now I take the time to grow a little taller
to hang over my own shadow like a gawky sunflower

CHIROPRACTOR

Time is a relative
Maybe a first cousin
Twisting to crack their back
At the dinner table

We will keep our spines aligned with our fancy
Silverware until nobody comes to dinner

Sometimes with
The lights off eyes closed I
Feel the continents shifting

A family of my own
Determining Earth's fate by seismology
Or geology
Or something
Or something else
Will take a long time

We will tell children to go to bed
And lean back on mattresses with never enough
Firmness
Or maybe it's softness
The continents will shift

And it will take so much longer for the mistakes to
Slip into the cracks
Of Earth's crust
Than it will to learn the names of new continents

Every 10 year old experiences time as a large
Hourglass plugged with wet sand
Back when adults looked to me like
Dry amphibians who had nothing to say

As I dry up
I curse the mattresses
That leaned back against me
As I slept on top of my baby teeth
And never felt the continents shifting

MAY

1

It's January and this year I want no more nightmares, but still some scary movies and still those camping trips on weekends where the trees smell cold and achy. I want to lose the rest of my teeth and stay up until 9 when the tooth fairy comes and I want the truth then, to be told that he is not real and that my teeth weren't for anybody to have except myself and I want the truth because I worry they are in a trash can gnawing at the corner of a McDonald's napkin and of course I do not want the truth at all.

3.

It's March and I want to start keeping a diary.

8

It's August and this year I want to get good grades without trying. I want to keep my backpack zipped up at the foot of my bed like an old dog and I don't want to write in a planner or take notes, but I want to be good. I want to sit up straight in class and not fall asleep and I don't want to do the work but I want the teachers to think I have done the work because I want to think I have done anything at all.

10

It's October and I want the news to stop talking about September 11th and everybody who is getting murdered by sharks in California and I want the news to make my parents happy at dinnertime and I want to be left alone to eat on the couch without setting down placemats.

1

It's January and this year I want to start keeping a diary.

12

It's December and I want to write in my diary more, or at least write in cursive like they do on TV and I want to write longer passages but my hand cramps up

and I want everyone to want to read my diary and I want to have the stamina to tell them no and not leave it open somewhere.

2

It's February and I want to lose my virginity before graduation

4

It's April and I want to lose my virginity in the least special way possible.

7

It's July and I want to lose my virginity before marriage, before I die, before anyone finds out that I'm a virgin.

12

It's December and I want to break up with him.

1

It's January and I want to stop masturbating to fan fiction from Battlestar Galactica.

1

It's January and I would be 26 in ten days but I'll be dead well before then.

3

It's March and I want to live again.

4

It's April and I don't want to lie another night on this couch if its cushions won't gulp me down with my greasy hair and dirty face and I want to be smothered and gone before anyone asks where I am.

1

It's January and I want someone to ask where I am.

9

It's September and I want people to stop talking about September 11th so much.

1

It's January and I want to start keeping a diary.

12

It's December and I want to be bad and reckless and dangerous and I want to stop wanting to be these things and start being these things and now I want another shot and I want whatever is on that table and I want whoever is in that bathroom and I want this person, this other person, to puppeteer my entire body until I go limp and the night is over.

It's morning and I want it to be night again.

1

It's January and I want it to be December again.

5

It's May and I want to live again.

Beth May

MY FATHER WRITES ABOUT HUNTING DOGS AND I HEAR HIS VOICE FOR THE FIRST TIME

My father and I meet
When I am five months old
Where we get our picture taken in front
Of an aircraft carrier
I keep the newspaper clipping
In a shoebox with some swim team ribbons

My father writes an article
In the ARIZONA WILDLIFE VIEWS newsletter
Where he lists our dead family dogs by name
Casey
Sandy
Bailey
Olive
He calls me his daughter
He calls my mother his wife
He remembers the first time he went hunting
He describes the freedom he feels now
Open air for miles
And a dog who loves him at his heel
He tells a newsletter what it all means to him

I write a poem in a book
Where I call my father my father
And I list ways I can understand him
And hide from all the ways I never will

I read an article my father wrote and I cry hard
At first for dead dogs
Then for knowing my father's thoughts
For the first time in many years
Understanding I may never know them again
Feeling five months old
Realizing I've never met him before

Afterword:
NOTIFICATIONS

A knock on my door
Fedex package for my neighbor
Health insurance bill for a woman who doesn't live
here any more
Probably because she is dead
Maybe because she couldn't pay for health insurance
Definitely in a era where health insurance companies
couldn't give less of a shit
Ship that bill to her kids
Shut her kids in their homes where they let every
unknown call go to voicemail

I pick up my phone I want to google
Do the police even knock on your door anymore?

I mean like in movies, when it's raining and your
parents are mad and you say angry words that
follow them out to their car and to the theater to the
restaurant where they pay the check and get back in
the car and smile, ready to forgive you, loving you
in a way you'll never hear because they're t-boned
by a truck whose driver is never named nor
punished and you don't know that until you open
the door and cops are there asking your name
Is it insane, that I think that's what it must be like?

I put down my phone

Is it insane that I wonder all the time about what my face would look like if my world fell apart and I still had to say "thank you officer thank you doctor they are dead but I guess I will live"

I pick up my phone I google
That one movie about the Army guys
Who tell people their soldiers are dead
Can't remember the name but- Ed Harris?
Oh yeah Woody Harrelson Oh yeah The Messenger

I put down my phone and think about every piece of bad news I've received off a human tongue.

My phone lights up and I am notified
that there is a domestic dispute on
Sepulveda and Airport I am notified that
Trevor from Hinge has responded to my
message I am notified that it's time for
me to drink water that it's time for me to
log into my diary app that it's been 3
days since my last entry and I'm really
fucking up my streak I'm notified that
Ruth Bader Ginsberg has died I am
notified that my period will start
tomorrow I am notified that cases of
Covid have risen in LA county I'm
notified that Sandra M is interested in
the used snowboard I am selling on
Facebook marketplace I am notified that
I need to drink water that there is a man

wielding a knife on 98th that Matt from
Hinge likes the picture of me in my
striped sweater that tomorrow is my
father's birthday that I should keep a
diary app or I might as well not exist.

My father will be 69 tomorrow and older than his
father ever was.

I put down my phone and try to remember the
moment he got the news, but I can't. Too long
ago. Barely remember the funeral. I remember
movies where the police knock on the door and
you're supposed to sink to the floor for a moment
before the plot carries on.

I remember hearing Kobe died the exact same way
that his family heard. Tabloids. Thoughts and
prayers. Carry on.

I wonder how long it will take for my plot to carry
on after I've lost someone truly irreplaceable.

How tough I should be.

How to address the mail of someone who isn't here
anymore.

THANK YOU

to the family I was born into, and the family I've picked up along the way. I love you!

SHOUT OUT

to John Bucher for giving me this opportunity

to Micah Bournes for giving me the confidence to accept this opportunity

to Myrlin Hepworth for showing me poetry could be cool

to Mr. Scrivener for teaching me I have a voice, and then giving that voice good grades despite its angst and phoniness

Beth May

ABOUT THE AUTHOR

Beth May is a writer and actor based in Los Angeles, CA. She writes scripts, poems, short stories, and tweets (@heybethmay). She also co-stars on "Dungeons & Daddies," a comedy D&D podcast.

Find some of her other works at:
www.etsy.com/shop/BethBooks

Follow her on Instagram/Twitter/TikTok:
@heybethmay

Or send her an email:
contactbethmay@gmail.com

And search **"Beth May"** on Youtube to hear some spoken word.

Printed in the USA
CPSIA information can be obtained
at www.ICGtesting.com
LVHW061554161123
763987LV00043B/124